*The Story of a Special Day*
Volume 129

# May
# 8

*The 128th day of the year (129th in leap years). There are 237 days remaining until the end of the year.*

by Michael Dobson

Timespinner
Press



This book is also available in e-book form for Kindle, e-pub devices, and other formats from your favorite online booksellers.

For more information about the series, about us, or about your special day, please email us at editor@timespinnerpress.com.

Look for other volumes in *The Story of a Special Day,* coming often. See www.timespinnerpress.com for details and for the most recent information.

# Table of Contents



**Cover:** A soda jerk (Photo: Alan Fisher, New York World-Telegram and Sun) and an early advetisement for Coca-Cola®. Coca-Cola® went on sale for the first time on May 8, 1886 — the COVER STORY and EVENT OF THE DAY.

# Quote of the Day

"A man who has nothing which he is willing to fight for, nothing which he cares more about than he does about his personal safety, is a miserable creature who has no chance of being free, unless made and kept so by the exertions of better men than himself."

John Stuart Mill, political philosopher and economist, died May 8, 1873

Today
in
History
May 8

A Coca-Cola® advertisement from the 1890s.

# What Happened on May 8?

## Cover Story/Event of the Day
## Coca-Cola® Goes on Sale

On May 8, 1886, at Jacob's Pharmacy in Atlanta, Georgia, the first Coca-Cola was sold. It cost 5¢. From that humble beginning, Coca-Cola has become a worldwide icon.

Coca-Cola began as a patent medicine. Pharmacist John Pemberton, who became addicted to morphine given to him after a saber wound to the chest received in the American Civil War, began experimenting with opium-free painkillers. His first attempt, French Wine Coca, combined cocaine with alcohol. With the passage of temperance legislation in Atlanta, he developed a non-alcoholic version, which he decided to market as a fountain drink instead of a medicine — although he still touted it as a cure for numerous diseases.

Financial problems caused Pemberton to sell his patent to Asa Candler, who founded the Coca-Cola Company. The company also changed Pemberton's formula, using "spent" coca leaves from which the cocaine has been removed and sold to pharmaceutical companies.

A combination of marketing genius and a franchise network of bottlers (the company only sold the syrup) built the company into a nationwide (and eventually worldwide brand. In 2013, it was available in more than 200 nations worldwide, with 1.8 billion Cokes® consumed each day.

*From the creation of great works of engineering and art, to devastating wars and natural disasters, thousands of years of history have left their mark on each and every day of the year. Here are some additional important events that occurred on May 8. (Illustrated items are shaded.)*

**1429** — In a critical turning point in the Hundred Years' War between England and France, **Joan of Arc** leads French forces in ending the Siege of Orléans.

*Jeanne d'Arc at the Siege of Orléans*, by Jules Eugène Lenepveu
(Photo: Tijmin Stam, CC BY-SA 2.5)

**1541** — Spanish conquistador Hernando de Soto becomes the **first European to reach the Mississippi** River.

*Discovery of the Mississippi by De Soto*, by William Henry Powell (Courtesy Architect of the Capitol)

**1861** — Richmond, Virginia, is named the **new capital of the Confederacy**, replacing Montgomery, Alabama.

**1877** — The first **Westminster Dog Show** takes place.

**1912** — The **Paramount Pictures** film studio is founded.

**1927** — French aviators **Nungesser and Coli** attempting to make the **first nonstop Paris to New York** trip, but disappear en route. They were competing for the same prize won by Lindbergh flying New York to Paris on May 20.

Postcard of *l'Oiseau Blanc* (*The White Bird*), flown by Charles Nungesser and Francois Coli in their 1927 transatlantic attempt

**1942** — In the first naval battle in which neither side's ships sighted the other, the **Battle of the Coral Sea** between Japan and a US/Australian force ends after four days.

**1945** — With the unconditional surrender of the Nazi government, **World War II in Europe ends**, known as Victory in Europe (V-E) Day. (*Also see page 37 and 38.*)

**1973** — A 71-day standoff between Federal authorities and American Indian Movement members at **Wounded Knee**, South Dakota, ends with the surrender of the militants.

**1978** — The first ascent of **Mount Everest** without supplemental oxygen is achieved.

**1980** — The World Health Organization announces the **eradication of smallpox**.

Members of the Canadian Women's Army Corps celebrate the end of World War II in Europe (Courtesy Galt Museum & Archives)

# Quote of the Day

"The people can never understand why the President does not use his powers to make them behave. Well all the president is, is a glorified public relations man who spends his time flattering, kissing, and kicking people to get them to do what they are supposed to do anyway."

Harry S. Truman, 33rd US President
born May 8, 1884

Births
and
Deaths
THE M
ACU
MAGNA
May 8

**Miguel Hidalgo**, leader in the Mexican War of Independence, lithograph by Luis Garcés. Miguel Hidalgo was born May 8, 1753.

# Notable May 8 People

*With the current world population at about seven billion people, on average about 19 million people also celebrate their birthdays on May 8 — and that isn't counting the millions and millions who came before! No matter when you were born, you share your birthday with many special people whose accomplishments (and occasionally embarrassments) have been noted as part of history.*

*In this section, you'll meet fascinating people who share your birthday. They're organized by what they're famous for, and then in reverse chronological order from most recent to earliest. Those who are shown in photographs or artwork have a box around them. We don't have photos of everyone, so please forgive us if your favorite person is missing.*

*Some of these people you've heard of, others may be new to you, but they all make up an important part of the reason that May 8 is a truly special day!*

Harry S. Truman

# Who Was Born on May 8?

## Person of the Day
## Harry S. Truman (1884)

Harry S. Truman, born May 8, 1884, became the 33rd President of the United States upon the death of Franklin Delano Roosevelt. He launched the Marshall Plan, established the Truman Doctrine to combat communism, and desegregated the military.

He spent his childhood on the family farm near Independence, Missouri. In World War I, he saw combat as an artillery officer in France. He briefly owned a haberdashery in Kansas City, and went into politics. He became a US senator in 1934, where he chaired the Truman Committee investigating waste and inefficiency in wartime contracts.

FDR died only four months into his last term, catapulting Truman to the presidency in the final months of World War II. His first major decision was to approve the use of nuclear weapons against Japan.

He ran for a full term in 1948 against former New York governor Thomas E. Dewey. In an upset victory, Truman triumphed and was elected to a term in his own right. During that term, he gained UN approval for the Korean War and made strides in the area of civil rights legislation.

Truman's presidency is rated by historians as "near great," ranking between 5th and 9th place among all who have held the office. He retired to Independence, Missouri, and died December 26, 1972.

## Art and Illustration

**Moebius (Jean Girard),** French artist and cartoonist who received worldwide acclaim for the *Blueberry* series, and for his contributions to numerous science fiction and fantasy films. *(1938)*

## Business and Society

**Friedrich Hayek,** economist and political philosopher who shared the 1974 Nobel Memorial Prize in Economics for his work in the theory of money and economic fluctuations; also known for his defense and advocacy of classical liberalism and for receiving the US Presidential Medal of Freedom in 1991. *(1899)*

**James H. Kindelberger,** aviation pioneer who led North American Aviation during the development of the X-15 and the XB-70; member of the International Aerospace Hall of Fame. *(1895)*

**Henry Dunant,** Swiss businessman and activist who founded the International Committee of the Red Cross and inspired the first Geneva Convention; first recipient of the Nobel Peace Prize. *(1828)*

## Government and Politics

**Ted Sorenson,** speechwriter and advisor to President John F. Kennedy; drafted Kennedy's inaugural address and is credited with major contributions to Kennedy's 1957 best-seller *Profiles in Courage. (1928)*

**Miguel Hidalgo,** Roman Catholic priest and military leader during the Mexican War of Independence. Although his campaign failed and he was executed, the war continued, leading to an independent Mexico. *(1753) (Photo page 10.)*

North American X-15, developed under the leadership of **James H. Kindelberger**

## Letters

**Roddy Doyle,** Irish novelist best known for his 1991 novel (later film) *The Commitments. (1958)*

**Peter Benchley,** novelist and screenwriter best known for his novel and screenplay for *Jaws. (1940)*

**Thomas Pynchon,** reclusive novelist best known for his novels *V, The Crying of Lot 49,* and *Gravity's Rainbow. (1929)*

**Sloan Wilson,** writer best known for his best sellers *The Man in the Gray Flannel Suit* (1955) and *A Summer Place* (1958), both adapted into movies. *(1920)*

**Thomas B. Costain,** historian and novelist who had several books adapted into film, including *The Black Rose* (1950) and *The Silver Chalice* (1954), the latter featuring the film debut of Paul Newman. *(1885)*

**Edward Gibbon,** historian best known for his six-volume work *The History of the Decline and Fall of the Roman Empire. (1737)*

## Music

**Enrique Iglesias,** Spanish singer-songwriter known as the "king of Latin pop." *(1975)*

**Alex Van Halen,** drummer and co-founder of Van Halen. *(1953)*

**Billy Burnette,** guitarist and singer known for his work with Fleetwood Mac. *(1953)*

**Chris Franz,** drummer for Talking Heads and the Tom Tom Club. *(1951)*

**Philip Bailey,** singer-songwriter known as an original member and lead singer of the band Earth, Wind, and Fire; member of the Rock and Roll Hall of Fame and the Songwriters Hall of Fame. *(1951)*

**Keith Jarrett,** jazz and classical pianist inducted into the *Down Beat* Hall of Fame *(1945)*

**Gary Glitter,** glam rock singer popular in the 1970s and 1980s. *(1944)*

**Paul Samwell-Smith,** founding member and bassist of The Yardbirds. *(1943)*

**John Fred,** singer best known for "Judy in Disguise (With Glasses)." *(1941)*

**Toni Tennille,** singer-songwriter best known as part of the musical duo Captain & Tennille, whose biggest hit was "Love Will Keep Us Together." *(1940)*

The Captain and Tennille (**Toni Tennille,** right; Daryl Dragon, left)

**Ricky Nelson,** singer-songwriter and actor who first came to fame as a member of the family sitcom The Adventures of Ozzie and Harriet; hit songs include "Poor Little Fool," "I'm Walkin'," and "Garden Party." *(1940)*

**Robert Johnson,** influential Delta blues singer-songwriter and guitarist elected to the Rock and Roll Hall of Fame. *(1911)*

**Red Nichols,** jazz cornettist and bandleader whose career was dramatized in the 1959 film *The Five Pennies,* starring Danny Kaye; member of the Big Band and Jazz Hall of Fame. *(1905)*

**Adolphe-Basile Routhier,** Canadian judge and lyricist who wrote the original version of the Canadian national anthem, "O Canada." *(1839)*

## Performing Arts

**Melissa Gilbert,** actress best known for playing Laura on the television series *Little House on the Prairie. (1964)*

**Stephen Furst,** actor who played "Flounder" in *Animal House,* Dr. Axelrod in *St. Elsewhere,* and Vir Cotto in *Babylon 5. (1954)*

**David Keith,** actor best known as Sid Worley in *An Officer and a Gentleman,* and for leading roles in *The Lords of Discipline* and *Firestarter. (1954)*

**Ricky Nelson** (left) with brother David Nelson from *The Adventures of Ozzie and Harriet*

**Miyoshi Umeki** (梅木 美代志), Japanese-American actress known for roles in the films *Sayonara*, *Flower Drum Song*, and *The Courtship of Eddie's Father*. *(1929)*

**Don Rickles,** stand-up comedian known as an "insult comic," actor in such films as *Run Silent, Run Deep*, and *Kelly's Heroes*, and the voice of Mr. Potato Head in *Toy Story* and its sequels. *(1926)*

Don Rickles

**Lex Barker,** actor best remembered for his five films as Tarzan. *(1919)*

**Bob Clampett,** animator, director, and puppetteer best known for his classic Warner Brothers cartoons and for the characters *Beany and Cecil*. *(1913)*

**Roberto Rossellini,** Italian director and screenwriter; husband of actress Ingrid Bergman and father of Isabella Rossellini. *(1906)*

**Arthur Q. Bryan,** comedian and voice actor best known for creating the voice of the cartoon character Elmer Fudd, and for his role as Dr. Gamble on the radio series *Fibber McGee and Molly. (1899)*

## Religion

**Fulton J. Sheen,** American Catholic archbishop who became one of the first and most famous radio and television preachers. *(1895)*

Bishop Fulton J. Sheen

## Science and Medicine

**H. Robert Horvitz,** biologist who shared the Nobel Prize in Physiology or Medicine for his research on the nematode worm. *(1947)*

**André Lwoff,** French microbiologist who received the Nobel Prize in Medicine or Physiology for the discovery of the mechanism that allowed some viruses to infect bacteria. *(1902)*

## Sports

**Bobby Labonte,** championship NASCAR driver who won the 200 Winston Cup series. *(1964)*

**Ronnie Lott,** cornerback and free safety for fourteen seasons in the NFL; member of the Pro Football Hall of Fame. *(1959)*

**Mike Cuellar,** starting pitcher for fifteen seasons in Major League Baseball, primarily for the Baltimore Orioles. *(1937)*

**Doug Atkins,** football defensive end for the University of Tennessee, the Cleveland Browns, the Chicago Bears, and the New Orleans Saints; member of the College Football Hall of Fame and the Pro Football Hall of Fame. *(1930)*

**Turkey Stearnes,** baseball outfielder with a career .344 batting average in the Negro leagues, member of the Baseball Hall of Fame. *(1901)*

**Edd Roush,** major league center fielder primarily with the Cincinnati Reds; member of the Baseball Hall of Fame. *(1893)*

**Francis Ouimet,** considered the "father of amateur golf" in the United States, first non-Briton elected Captain of the Royal and Ancient Golf Club of St. Andrews, member of the World Golf Hall of Fame. *(1893)*

**Dan Brouthers,** first baseman recognized as the first great slugger in baseball history; member of the Baseball Hall of Fame. *(1858)*

1888 baseball card of Dan Brouthers

**Ross Barnes,** baseball player who hit the first home run in the National League, established numerous batting records with the league. *(1850)*

*Te Faaturuma* by Paul Gauguin (1891)

# Who Died on May 8?

## Art and Photography

**Maurice Sendak,** illustrator and writer of children's books, best known for *Where The Wild Things Are.* *(2012)*

**Iain Macmillan,** photographer best known for taking the cover photograph for the Beatles' *Abbey Road* album. *(2006)*

**Garth Williams,** artist best known as the illustrator of children's classics including *Stuart Little, Charlotte's Web,* and the *Little House* series. *(1996)*

**Paul Gauguin,** influential French post-Impressionist artist best known for his paintings of Tahitian life. *(1903)*

## Business

**Charles "Bebe" Rebozo,** Florida banker and businessman best known as a friend and confidant of US President Richard Nixon. *(1998)*

**Neil Bogart,** founded the Casablanca Records label. *(1982)*

**William Fox,** motion picture executive best known for founding the Fox Film Corporation. *(1952)*

**Harry Gordon Selfridge,** American retailer best known for founding the London-based Selfridges department store. *(1947)*

## Government

**Kamehameha I the Great,** unified the Hawaiian islands as founder and first ruler of the Kingdom of Hawai'i. *(1819*)*

Kamehameha I

---

* Some sources list the day of his death as May 14, 1819.

# Letters

**Bud Shrake,** writer best known for co-writing *Harvey Penick's Little Red Book* of golf advice, the best-sellling sports book in publishing history. *(2009)*

**Avram Davidson,** award-winning writer and editor of fantasy, science fiction, and crime fiction. *(1993)*

**Robert A. Heinlein,** often called the "dean of science fiction writers," whose notable works include *Stranger in a Strange Land* and *Starship Troopers.* *(1988)*

**Robert Heinlein**, L. Sprague de Camp, and Isaac Asimov

**Theodore Sturgeon,** American science fiction and fantasy writer best known for his 1953 novel *More Than Human;* member of the Science Fiction and Fantasy Hall of Fame. *(1985)*

**Gustave Flaubert,** influential French novelist best known for his 1857 novel *Madame Bovary. (1880)*

Gustave Flaubert

## Music

**Eddy Arnold,** country music singer and member of the Grand Ole Opry; elected to the Country Music Hall of Fame. *(2008)*

Eddy Arnold

**Rudolf Serkin,** classical pianist known for his interpretation of Beethoven's works; received the Presidential Medal of Freedom and the National Medal of Arts for his achievements. *(1991)*

## Performing Arts

**Bryan Forbes,** directed such films as *The Stepford Wives, Séance on a Wet Afternoon,* and *King Rat. (2013)*

**Jeanne Cooper,** actress best known for her forty-year run as Katherine Chancellor on the daytime drama *The Young and the Restless*; mother of actor Corbin Bernsen. *(2013)*

**Dana Plato,** actress best known for her role as Kimberly on the sitcom *Diff'rent Strokes*; died from a drug overdose after a long struggle with poverty and substance abuse. *(1999)*

**Dirk Bogarde,** actor known for such films as *Death in Venice, The Night Porter,* and *A Bridge Too Far. (1999)*

**George Peppard**, film and television actor best known for films including *The Blue Max* and for his role as "Hannibal" Smith in the 1980s television series *The A-Team. (1994)*

## Religion and Philosophy

**Oswald Spengler,** German philosopher of history best known for his book *The Decline of the West. (1936)*

**Helena Blavatsky (Елена Блаватска),** Russian occultist and spirit medium who founded the esoteric religion known as Theosophy. *(1880) (See also page 42.)*

**John Stuart Mill,** philosopher and political economist who made major contributions to social and political theory and to the development of the scientific method. First member of the British Parliament to call for women's suffrage. *(1873) (Photo page 33)*

George Peppard in *The Blue Max* (1966)

## Science

**Roger L. Easton,** physicist and principal inventor and designer of the Global Positioning System (GPS). *(2014)*

**Antoine Lavoisier,** French nobleman and pioneering chemist often called the "father of modern chemistry." First identified the role oxygen played in combustion, helped construct the metric system, and wrote the first list of elements. He was beheaded during the French Revolution for selling adulterated tobacco. *(1794)*

Antoine Lavoisier

John Stuart Mill

# Quote of the Day

"If they can get you asking the wrong questions, they don't have to worry about answers."

Thomas Pynchon, novelist
born May 8, 1937

Holidays
Around
the World
May 8

*The Stars and Stripes* military newspaper front page for May 8, 1945, celebrating the end of World War II in Europe

# May 8 Holidays and Celebrations

*If you're looking for a reason to take your special day off, you should know that every single day is a holiday somewhere in the world! Here's some of what you can celebrate on May 8!*

## Victory in Europe Day (Allied nations)

On May 8, 1945, the Allies formally accepted the unconditional surrender of Nazi Germany, marking the end of World War II in Europe. This celebration, known as V-E Day, is celebrated in the US and in many European nations.

Nations that made up the former Soviet Union and other Eastern Bloc nations observe Victory Day on May 9, because it was May 9 Moscow time when the German military surrender became effective.

May 8 and May 9 together are also celebrated as the Time of Remembrance and Reconcilitation for Those Who Lost Their Lives During the Second World War by resolution of the United Nations General Assembly.

A number of nations observe V-E Day under a variety of names. In France, it's *Victoire 1945*, Poland observes *Narodowy Dzień Zwycięstwa*, the Czech Republic *Den osvobození*, and Slovakia *Deň víťazstva nad fašizmom*.

## General Events

### Emancipation Day (Columbus, Mississippi)
The date on which African-American enslaved people were emancipated varied by location. In Columbus, Mississippi, the "Eighth o'May" commemorates the date in 1865 when African-Americans in eastern Mississippi learned of their freedom. (Although Federal law outlawed slavery in Mississippi in 1865, the state of Mississippi didn't ratify the Constitutional amendment abolishing slavery until February 2013.)

### Eobeoinal (어버이날) (South Korea)
Many nations set aside a day to honor parents. In South Korea, Parent's Day is celebrated on May 8.

### Furry Dance/Flora Day (Helston, Cornwall)
To celebrate the passing of winter and the arrival of spring, the community of Helston, in Cornwall, United Kingdom, continues to celebrate one of the oldest British customs still practiced today.

Every year on May 8 (or the Saturday before if the 8th falls on Sunday or Monday), three dances are held: a children's dance in the morning, a midday dance at noon, and an evening dance. Dancers wear Lilies of the Valley and dress in traditional formal clothes. Over a thousand people participate. A pageant, the *Hal-an-Tow*, a mystery play with historical and mythological themes, takes place around the town.

In spite of the name, people don't wear fur — the name comes from the local pronunciation of "fair."

Furry Dancers in Helston (Photo: Steve G, CC B-SA 2.0)

## Natalicio de Miguel Hidalgo (Mexico)

In Mexico, the 1753 birthday of Miguel Hidalgo, initiator of the Mexican Independence War, is celebrated on May 8. *(Photo page 10)*

## Truman Day (Missouri)

On May 8, the state of Missouri celebrates the birthday of the only US president to come from that state, Harry S. Truman. (See the "Person of the Day.") *(Photo page 12)*

## Veterandagen (Norway)

Many nations set aside a day each year to honor military veterans. In Norway, Veteran's Day is celebrated on May 8, in honor of the end of World War II in Europe.

## World Red Cross and Red Crescent Day (international)

The International Red Cross and Red Crescent movement celebrates the birthday of its founder and recipient of the first Nobel Peace Prize, Henry Dunant, on May 8, 1828.

# Religious Feast Days and Holidays

### Easter

The Christian holiday of Easter in Western Christianity is held on the first Sunday after the Paschal Full Moon following the March equinox, which is officially set at March 21 by church reckoning. Easter can therefore occur as early as March 22 and as late as April 25, but occurs most often in April.

In Eastern Christianity, which uses the Julian calendar, Easter occurs between April 4 and May 8. (See "What Day of the Week is May 8?" for more information about the differences between the Gregorian and the Julian calendars.)

Easter celebrates the resurrection of Jesus Christ on the third day after his crucifixion. In the liturgical calendar, Easter follows the season of Lent, and begins the period known as Eastertide, which ends on Pentecost Sunday. Easter is observed religiously in a morning service.

*La crucifixión* by El Greco

## Saint Days

*Each day in the year is considered a feast day for one or more saints. They are somewhat different in western Christianity (Catholicism and many forms of Protestantism) and in eastern (Orthodox) Christianity. There are many others; this is a selection.*

In *Western Christianity*, May 8 is the feast day of Amato Ronconi, Arsenius the Great, Desideratus, Julian of Norwich (Anglican and Lutheran Church), Magdalene of Canossa, and Peter of Tarentaise.

In *Eastern Orthodox Christianity*, it is also the commemoration of the Apostle John, Augustina the Martyr, Agathius, Emilia, Hierax of Egypt, Milles the Melodist, Hellandius of Auxerre, Gybrian, Iduberga, Benedict II, Wiro and Plechelm, Macarius of Ghent, Pimen the Faster, and Arsenius of the Kiev Caves. (These saints are honored on April 25 by "Old Calendrists.†")

## White Lotus Day (Theosophy)

The Western esoteric movement known as Theosophy observes the anniversary of the death of its founder Helena Petrovna Blavatsky on May 8, 1891. *(See also page 30.)*

---

† "Old Calendrists" use the older Julian calendar rather than the modern Gregorian calendar for liturgical purposes. April 13 on the Julian calendar is the same day as March 31 on the Gregorian calendar. For more about the different types of calendars, see "What Day of the Week is April 13?"

## Food Holidays

*In the United States, almost every day of the year is dedicated to a particular food — some days honor more than one!. Sponsored by manufacturers, retailers, farmers, or simply fans, these days are often proclaimed by the President, Congress, state governors, or mayors.*

In the US, May 8 is **National Coconut Cream Pie Day.** Cream pies come in many types: vanilla, lemon, lime, peanut butter, banana, chocolate, and (today) coconut — but always topped with whipped cream!

Cream pies are a common gimmick in comedy routines that end up with the pie in someone's face. In movies, cream pies are generally made entirely of whipped cream, or (to save money) shaving cream. "Pieing," or throwing a pie at someone who isn't part of the act, can be punished as assault.

A slice of coconut cream pie from Chicago's Golden Nugget Restaurant (Photo: Kim Scarborough, CC BY-SA 2.5)

***Honorary Food Months:*** *In addition, the entire month of May is used to celebrate numerous foods. Here's a list of food-related observances in the month of May!*

- National Beef Month
- National Barbecue Month
- National Loaded Potato Month
- National Chocolate Custard Month
- Month National Egg Month
- National Hamburger Month
- National Salad Month
- National Salsa Month
- National Strawberry Month
- National Raisin Week (first week in May)
- National Herb Week (first week in May)

The first Saturday in May is also **National Homebrew Day**. Bottoms up!

Home beer brewing (Photo: Makyo, CC BY-SA 3.0)

## Honorary Months

*Presidents, Congresses, and nations around the world issue proclamations recognizing particular months to honor certain causes. These events generally fall in May, though honorary months do come and go.*

*Three places to get up to date information are Wikipedia, the current edition of Chase's* Calendar of Events *or the website Brownielocks. Here are some honorary designations for May.*

- Asian Pacific American Heritage Month
- Better Hearing and Speech Month
- Celiac Awareness Month
- Community Action Awareness Month (North Dakota)
- Cystic Fibrosis Awareness Month
- Ehlers-Danlos Syndrome Awareness Month
- Flores de Mayo (Philippines)
- Garden for Wildlife Month
- Haitian Heritage Month
- Hepatitis Awareness Month
- International Mediterranean Diet Month
- Jewish American Heritage Month
- Kaamatan harvest festival
- Mental Health Awareness Month
- Month of the Blessed Virgin Mary. (Catholicism)
- National ALS Awareness Month
- National Brain Tumor Awareness Month
- National Corps Member Appreciation Month
- National Electrical Safety Month (United States)

- National Foster Care Month (United States)
- National Golf Month
- National Innovators Month
- National Military Appreciation Month
- National Mobility Awareness Month (United States, Canada)
- National Moving Month
- National Osteoporosis Month
- National Pet Month (United Kingdom)
- National Smile Month (United Kingdom)
- National Stroke Awareness Month
- National Water Safety Month
- New Zealand Music Month (New Zealand)
- Older Americans Month
- Season of Emancipation (April 14 to August 23) (Barbados)
- Skin Cancer Awareness Month
- South Asian Heritage Month (International)
- World Trade Month

## Moveable and Multi-Day Events

*Some events take place over a specific week or time period. Start and finish dates may vary from year to year. Some events occur on different days each year (such as "fourth Saturday of a month"). These events sometimes take place on or include May 8.*

**Second Sunday in May**
- Children's Day (Spain)

- Father's Day (Romania)
- Mother's Day (United States and others)
- State Flag and State Emblem Day (Belarus)
- World Fair Trade Day (international)

**First Full Week in May**

- National Teacher Appreciation Week (US)
- Occupational Safety and Health Week (US)

**Second Week in May**

- Green Office Week (UK)
- National Arbour Week (Ontario)
- National Hurricane Preparedness Week (US)
- National Nursing Week (US)
- National Stuttering Awareness Week (US)
- Sign Language Week (New Zealand)

# Just for Fun

*Anybody can make up a holiday, and many people do! While none of these are officially recognized and some may come and go, here are a few more holidays for May 8.*

- No Socks Day
- Motorcycle Mass and Blessing of the Bikes Day (first Sunday)
- World Laughter Day (first Sunday)
- World Naked Gardening Day (first Saturday)

# Quote of the Day

"Rough winds do shake the
darling buds of May."

William Shakespeare, Sonnet XVIII

49

"May," from the *Brevarium Grimani* by Simon Bening (c.1510)

# May: The Fifth Month

*"Then came fair May, the fairest maid on ground,*
*Deck'd all with dainties of the season's pride,*
*And throwing flowers out of her lap around. ."*

— Edward Spenser, *The Faerie Queene, Book VII*

According to many scholars, the month of May takes its name from the Roman goddess Maia, an earth goddess who was the mother of Mercury. The poet Ovid, on the other hand, claimed that May took its name from the Latin maiores, meaning ancestors. In either case, the month of May in ancient Rome was marked by sacrifices to Maia, and her son Mercury was honored on the Ides of May (May 15).

May is the fifth month of the year in both Julian and Gregorian calendars. It was originally the third month in ancient Rome, because the new year began on March 1. Although Julius Caesar changed the length of several months during his great calendar reform (the Julian calendar), the length of May has remained constant at 31 days.

In the northern hemisphere, May occurs in the springtime, and in the southern hemisphere, May takes place in fall. Strangely, no other month begins or ends on the same day of the week as the beginning or ending of May, although January of the following year always begins and ends on the same day of the week as this year's May.

# May in Other Cultures

*The month of April has different names in different languages. Some nations use calendars other than the Gregorian, and their months may overlap with April. Still, they often have a word for April itself.*

- In Latin and Old English, the month of May was named *Maius*, and it is *Mai* in French.

- In Arabic, the month is مايو, pronounced *māyū*.

- In Chinese, the equivalent month is 五月.

- Croatians call the month *svibanj* and in Czech it is *květen*. In Finland, it is *toukokuu*.

- The Jewish month of *Sivan* (סִיוָן) normally falls in May-June.

- It is the third month of the Jewish ecclesiastical year.

- The Irish called the month *bealtaine,* and it marked the beginning of summer.

- Slovenians call May *veliki traven,* or the month of the big grass.

# May Sayings and Superstitions

*Here are some sayings and superstitions associated with the month of May.*

Never buy a broom in May.

"Wash a blanket in May / Wash a dear one away."

Cats born in May will bring snakes into the house.

"Those who bathe in May / Will soon be laid in clay."

## Marriage in May

May is an unlucky month for getting married.

"Marry in May and rue the day, but marry in April if you can, joy for maiden and for man."

Which day? "Monday for wealth, Tuesday for health, Wednesday the best day of all, Thursday for losses, Friday for crosses, Saturday for no luck at all."

# May Symbols

**Birthstone:** Emerald

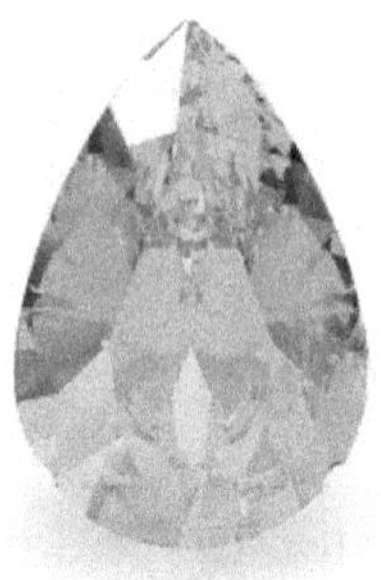

**Birth Flowers:** Lily of the Valley and Hawthorn

Lily of the Valley

Common Hawthorn

"May," by Eugène Grasset

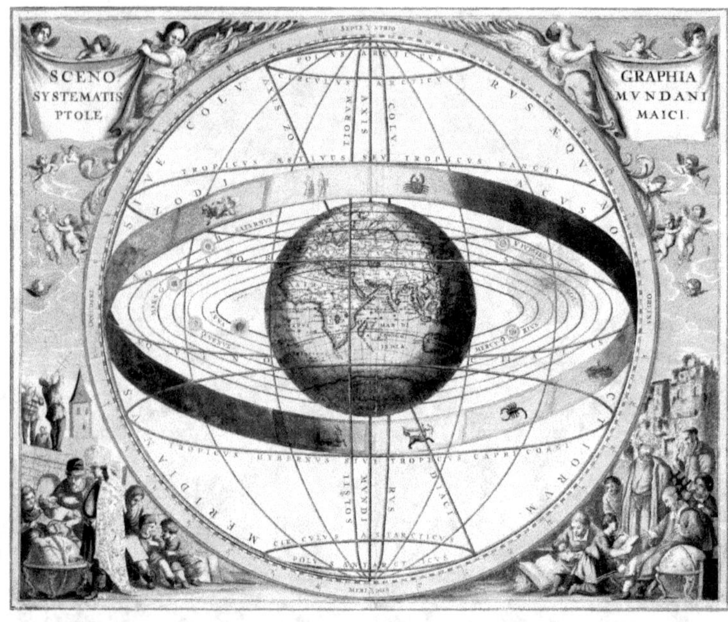

*Scenography of the Ptolemaic Cosmography,* by Johannes van Loon, based on Andreas Cellarius's *Harmonia Macrocosmica*, 1660

# May 8 Zodiac Signs

From the perspective of someone on Earth, the Sun appears to move through the sky throughout the year, along a path astronomers call the *ecliptic plane*. The ecliptic plane is divided into twelve constellations, known as the zodiac, based on traditionally observed patterns of stars. On your birthday, you can't see your constellation, because it's in the daytime sky.

The zodiac was first developed by Babylonian astronomers about 2,500 years ago. Because they were unaware that the Earth wobbles like a spinning top (known as *precession*), they didn't make allowance for the fact that the Sun's path through the zodiac changes over time.

That means there are now two sets of dates for your birth sign. The *tropical dates* are the original Babylonian dates; the *sidereal dates* tell you where the Sun actually appears as it moves along its annual path.

For May 8, the tropical sign is **Taurus** and the sidereal sign is **Aries.**

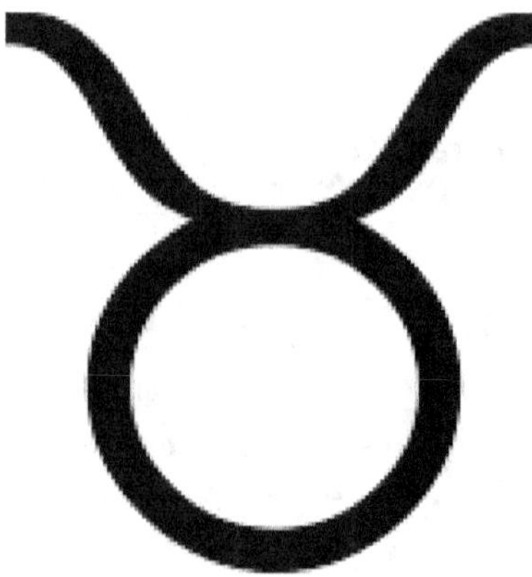

# Taurus

**Tropical** April 21 to May 21
**Sidereal** May 16 to June 15

The astrological sign of Taurus (the Bull) originated in ancient Mesopotamia, who called it the "Bull of Heaven," and believed it to be a symbol of strong will, perseverance, and determination. The Egyptians knew it as Hathor (the Cow Goddess), who was the goddess of beauty, love, and happiness. That's why Roman astrologers said that Taurus was ruled by Venus, their goddess of beauty.

In astrology, Taurus is an Earth sign, compatible with Cancer, Capricorn, and Pisces. Taureans are supposed to be headstrong, powerful, and hard-working.

# Aries

**Tropical** March 21 to April 19
**Sidereal** April 15 to May 15

In Greek mythology, Aries is a ram with golden wings and golden wool who rescued the twins Phrixus and Helle from certain death. Although Helle died in the rescue attempt, the grateful Phrixus sacrificed the ram to Zeus. The golden fleece from the sacrificed ram played a prominent part in the later myth of Jason and the Argonauts.

In astrology, Aries, a fire sign, is compatible with the other fire signs of Gemini, Leo, and Sagittarius, and to a lesser extent with air signs Scorpio and Libra. Arians are supposed to be adventurous, enthusiastic, quick-tempered, and impulsive.

Illustration by Edward Penfield

# What Day of the Week is May 8?

On what day of the week does May 8 fall?

Surprisingly, this isn't an easy question. Because the calendar year is 365 days long (366 in leap years), it doesn't divide evenly by the seven days of the week.

Also, the Earth goes around the Sun in about 365-1/4 days, so a calendar tends to drift over time. That's why the same date falls on different weekdays in different years.

This is made even more complicated by a change in calendars that took place in 1582. Our modern calendar has its roots in ancient Rome, in a calendar reform conducted by Julius Caesar. Caesar commissioned mathematicians to attack the problem, and they came up with the idea of leap years, and thus standardized the calendar for centuries to come. This was called the Julian calendar.

Over time, however, the small errors in Caesar's calculation compounded. That's why Pope Gregory XIII commissioned the Gregorian calendar, used in most of the world today. Some countries converted in 1582, when the calendar was first developed; some converted later; other still haven't changed.

Gregorian and Julian aren't the only types of calendars. The Hebrew year, the Islamic year, and many other calendars are used in different parts of the world and among different people.

You can convert Gregorian dates to other calendars, including the Hebrew calendar, the Islamic calendar, and even the Mayan calendar by visiting the Fourmilab Calendar Converter at http://www.fourmilab.ch/documents/calendar/.

Chinese calendar systems are quite complex and have changed several times; a full discussion is far beyond the scope of this book. If you're interested, you can find information here: http://www.hermetic.ch/cal_stud/chinese_cal.htm.

# On Names and Dates

Historians use "CE" (Common Era) and "BCE" (Before the Common Era) instead of the more common "AD" (Anno Domini, or Year of Our Lord) and "BC" (Before Christ), reflecting the fact that the year-numbering system established by the Gregorian calendar is used throughout the world in many countries not culturally Christian.

The CE/BCE designation dates back to at least 1708, and has been adopted as a standard by the United Nations and the Universal Postal Union. Because this series of books covers events and people of all nations and cultures, we use the CE/BCE terms.

The abbreviation "O.S." ("Old Style") and "N.S." ("New Style") on some dates refers to the fact that the Russian Empire (in particular) did not switch from the Julian to the Gregorian calendar at the same time as the rest of Europe, and therefore some figures and events have two dates.

Also, in the Julian calendar in England in the 16th century, the year began on March 25 rather than January 1. To avoid confusion with Gregorian dates, dates between January and March were often written using both years.

People and events whose original names are not in the Western alphabet have their native names (where possible) in the appropriate script shown in parenthesis. If you are using an e-reader to access an electronic version of this book, all characters don't always display on all devices.

A 50-year brass perpetual calendar.

# Quote of the Day

"Time is an illusion, lunchtime doubly so."

Douglas Adams,
from *The Hitchhiker's Guide to the Galaxy*

Notes
and
Credits
Timespinner
Press

Cartoon by John T. McCutcheon

# Copyright, Credit, and Contact

## Follow Us

Our blog "This Day in History" (http://
timespinnerpress.com/this-day-in-history/) features short
articles on events and people associated with each day, and
updates several times each week. Also subscribe to the
"Quote of the Day" at http://timespinnerpress.com/quote-
of-the-day/. You can get daily links by following us on
Facebook at TimespinnerPress, or on Twitter as
@sidewisethinker.

## Contact Us

Find an error or a format problem? Want information about
the series, about us, or about when the volume for your
special day might be available? Please email us at
editor@timespinnerpress.com. (We also take requests if your
special day isn't yet complete. Please give us at least six
weeks' notice if possible.)

## Sources

We owe a great debt to Wikipedia, which is our first stop for
research. We attempt to make independent confirmation of
all important dates and facts through a variety of other
sources.

Other sources we frequently use include the Library of
Congress; "on this day" listings from *Encyclopedia Britannica*,
the *New York Times*, and the BBC; Omniglot for the names of
months in other languages; *Chase's Calendar of Events*; and, of
course, the always essential Google.

All art and photographs are either in the public domain, used under a Creative Commons license, or with a "fair use" justification, and most frequently come from Wikimedia Commons and the Library of Congress Prints and Photographs Division.

Attribution is provided where possible, or as requested by the copyright owner, or when there is particular historical significance, listed below. For information about any particular illustration or photograph, please contact us.

# Credits

1.  The 1936 photograph of a soda jerk used on the front cover was taken by Alan Fisher, and is part of the New York *World-Telegram and Sun* collection at the Library of Congress (digital ID cph.3c13825). Per the instrument of gift, all photographs in that collection are in the public domain.

2.  The Coca-Cola® advertisement used on the front cover is in the public domain because it was created prior to January 1, 1923.

3.  The illustration of the month of May used on the back cover is from the French Gothic illuminated manuscript *Les Très Riches Heures du duc de Berry* by the Limbourg Brothers, Jean Colombe, and an intermediate painter whose name is lost to history. It is in the public domain because its copyright has expired.

4.  The box graphic used on the first page is from a 1916 pamphlet entitled "Divorce versus Democracy" authored by G. K. Chesterton, originally published in London by the Society of St. Peter and St. Paul. It is in the public domain in the US because it was published prior to 1923, and is in the public domain in all countries (including the country of origin) in which the copyright time is the author's life plus 70 years or less.

5.  The graphic design for the section pages in this book is from a design originally created for a pharmacy label. It is courtesy of Wellcome Images (ICV No 11073, photo V0010813), and is used here under CC BY-SA 4.0.

6.    The advertisement for Coca-Cola® was created circa 1890 and is in the public domain because its copyright hase expired. It is from the collection of the Library of Congress, digital ID cph.3g12222.

7.    The painting of Joan of Arc at the Siege of Orléans by Jules Eugène Lenepveu was created prior to 1898, and is in the public domain because its copyright has expired. The photograph of the painting was taken by Tijmin Stam, who has made it available under CC BY-SA 2.5.

8.    The painting *Discovery of the Mississippi by De Soto* by William Henry Powell was created prior to 1879 and is in the public domain because its copyright has expired. It is in the collection of the US Capitol and can be seen in the Capitol Rotunda.

9.    The 1927 postcard of the aircraft *l'Oiseau Blanc* flown by Charles Nungesser and Francois Coli is in the public domain in the European Union because it is more than 70 years old, and in the United States because it was first published in the United States between 1923 and 1977 without a copyright notice.

10.   The 1945 photograph of the Canadian Women's Army Corps celebrating V-E Day is courtesy Galt Museum and Archives, image P19891053019. According to the Galt Museum, there are no known copyright restrictions on this photograph.

11.   The 1873 lithograph of Miguel Hidalgo by Luis Garcés is in the public domain because its copyright has expired.

12.   The photograph of Harry S. Truman is in the public domain as a work created by an employee of the US government as part of his or her official duties. Courtesy National Archives and Records Administration, NAID 530677.

13.   The 1960 photograph of the X-15 is in the public domain as a work solely created by NASA. The X-15 in the picture can be seen at the Smithsonian's National Air and Space Museum, Washington DC.

14.   The 1976 publicity photograph of the Captain and Tennille is in the public domain because it was first published in the United States between 1923 and 1977 without a copyright notice. Traditionally, publicity photographs are not copyrighted because of the way in which they are intended to be used.

15. The 1959 publicity photograph from *The Adventures of Ozzie and Harriet* is in the public domain because it was first published in the United States between 1923 and 1977 without a copyright notice.

16. The 1973 publicity photograph of Don Rickles is in the public domain because it was first published in the United States between 1923 and 1977 without a copyright notice.

17. The 1956 publicity photograph of Fulton J. Sheen is in the public domain because it was first published in the United States between 1923 and 1977 without a copyright notice.

18. The 1888 baseball card of Dan Brouthers is from the Benjamin K. Edwards collection at the Library of Congress, digital ID bbc.0556f. It is in the public domain because its copyright has expired.

19. The 1891 painting *Te Faaturuma* by Paul Gauguin is in the public domain because its copyright has expired. It is from the collection of the Worcester Art Museum, Massachusetts, and made available through The Yorck Project.

20. The 1810 painting of Kamehameha I is courtesy Hawaii State Archives. It is in the public domain because its copyright has expired.

21. The 1944 photograph of Robert Heinlein, Isaac Asimov, and L. Sprague de Camp at the Philadelphia Navy Yard is in the public domain as a work created by an employee of the US government as part of that person's official duties.

22. The photograph of Gustave Flaubert was taken prior to 1880, and is in the public domain because its copyright has expired.

23. The 1964 publicity photograph of Eddy Arnold is in the public domain because it was first published in the United States between 1923 and 1977 without a copyright notice.

24. The 1966 publicity photograph of George Peppard in *The Blue Max* is in the public domain because it was first published in the United States between 1923 and 1977 without a copyright notice.

25. The illustration of John Stuart Mill first appeared in *Popular Science Monthly* in 1872 or 1873. It is in the public domain because its copyright has expired.

26. The illustration of Antoine Lavoisier was created prior to 1900. It is in the public domain because its copyright has expired.

27. The front page of the May 8, 1945, issue of *Stars and Stripes* is in the public domain as a work created by employees of the US government as part of their official duties.

28. The 1993 photograph of dancers on Flora Day was taken by Steve G, and is used here under CC BY-SA 2.0.

29. The painting *La crucifixión* by El Greco is located in the Museo del Prado. It is in the public domain because its copyright has expired.

30. The 2005 photograph of a coconut cream pie was taken by Kim Scarborough, and is used here under CC BY-SA 2.5.

31. The 2010 photograph of a beer hombrewing setup was taken by Makyo, and is used here under CC BY-SA 3.0.

32. The painting "May" by Simon Bening is from the *Brevarium Grimani,* circa 1510, and is in the public domain because its copyright has expired.

33. The 1815 woodcut of a proposal is in the public domain because its copyright has expired.

34. The photograph of an emerald was taken by Les Facettes and is used here under the CC BY-SA 3.0 license.

35. The photograph of a lily of the valley (*convallaria majalis*) is by H. Zell and is used here under the CC BY-SA 3.0 license.

36. The photograph of a hawthorn (*Crataegus monogyna*) is by Sannse and is used here under the CC BY-SA 3.0 license.

37. The 1896 drawing "May" by Eugène Grasset is in the public domain because its copyright has expired.

38. The celestial sphere is from *Scenography of the Ptolemaic Cosmography*, by Johannes van Loon, based on Andreas Cellarius's *Harmonia Macrocosmica*, 1660. It is in the public domain because its copyright has expired.

39. The 1906 automobile calendar is by Edward Penfield, and is in the collection of the Library of Congress Prints and Photographs Division. It is in the public domain because its copyright has expired.

40. The 50-year perpetual calendar photograph is in the public domain.

41. The cartoon by John T. McCutcheon is from his 1905 collection *The Mysterious Stranger and Other Cartoons by John T. McCutcheon.* It is in the public domain because its copyright has expired.

42. The painting "May" by Hans Thoma is from his book *Festkalender.* It is in the public domain because it was published prior to 1923 and its copyright has expired.

## License Description and Terms

Aside from material purely in the public domain, photographs and other material in this book are used under specific licenses permitting free use, usually with an attribution requirement. For full text and terms of these licenses, click or enter the appropriate links below. If you believe there is an error in the copyright status or attribution of any of these images, please email us.

- Creative Commons Attribution 2.0 Generic (CC-BY 2.0): http://creativecommons.org/licenses/by/2.0/deed.en
- Creative Commons Attribution-Share Alike 3.0 Generic (CC-BY-SA 3.0): http://creativecommons.org/licenses/by-sa/3.0/
- Creative Commons Attribution-Share Alike 2.5 Generic (CC-BY-SA 2.5): http://creativecommons.org/licenses/by-sa/2.5/deed.en
- Creative Commons Attribution-Share Alike 2.0 Generic (CC-BY-SA 2.0): http://creativecommons.org/licenses/by/2.0/deed.en
- Creative Commons Attribution-Share Alike 1.0 Generic (CC-BY-SA 1.0): http://creativecommons.org/licenses/by-sa/1.0/deed.en
- CC0 1.0 Universal (CC0 1.0) Public Domain Dedication (CC0 1.0) http://creativecommons.org/publicdomain/zero/1.0/deed.en
- GNU Free Documentation License (GFDL): http://en.wikipedia.org/wiki/Wikipedia:Text_of_the_GNU_Free_Documentation_License
- License Art Libre (Free Art License): http://artlibre.org

# Other Books from Timespinner Press

### *The Story of a Special Day*
*Michael Dobson*

A series of (eventually) 366 volumes covering everything that happened on your special day! Events, births, deaths, quotes, holidays, and much more. It's like a birthday card they'll never throw away!

US$7.95 print/US$2.99 ebook.

### *From Plassey to Pakistan*
*Humayun Mirza*

The history of British Colonial India and the formation of Pakistan from the unique perspective of the son of Pakistan's first president and last of the royal line of Bengal, Bihar, and Orissa! This unique historical document tells the inside story of this distinguished family, including the detailed story of the coup that toppled his father from power!

US$27.95 print

## *A Whole New Navy: America's War in the Pacific*

*Miles Durr*

The most comprehensive and detailed description of America's naval war in the Pacific ever—every battle, every ship, every task force and every task group from Pearl Harbor through the Japanese surrender! A must-have for the collection of every World War II buff!

US$29.95 print

## *Improbable History: The Weird, the Obscure, and the Strangely Important*

*edited by Michael Dobson*

From the birth of Western civilization to the rescue of Apollo 13, from the Leaning Tower of Pisa to Florence's Duomo, history has often turned on small, improbable details. Whatever happened to the ancient Samaritan people? Why did a fortuitous rainstorm allow the British to conquer India? How did an air raid in Italy lead to the development of chemotherapy? What happened when Albert Einstein met Adolf Hitler on the streets of Berlin? How did the Japanese manage to attack the US mainland using balloons? A cast of award-winning writers tackle some of the strangest tales in history!

US$19.95 print

### *The Letters of William Philip Schwartz 1842-1855*

*edited by John F. Schwartz*

The 19th century soldier and adventurer William Philip Schwartz wrote a series of vivid and detailed letters chronicling his adventures in the Indian Wars, the Mexican-American War, the Gold Rush, and his term as Marine sergeant aboard the USS Constellation. A pioneer in photography, he took *the first known war photographs*. An unforgettable first-hand look into life in the 19th century!

US$17.95 print

Timespinner
Press

www.timespinnerpress.com

May, by Hans Thoma